AF484664

FATHERHOOD

VICTOR D.
RODGERS JR.

FATHERHOOD

THE SHORTENED
STORY

Marie Lynn LLC

CONTENTS

CONTENTS

ABOUT MY HOOD

FATHERHOOD is a collection of experiences and stories from the perspective of a loving, respectable, God fearing, praying, driven, flawed, but resilient man named Dad. Dad offers insight about his life; his transition to FATHERHOOD, the ups, downs, surround sound so loud, was sure he'd drown. FATHERHOOD is the opportunity to see through your lens and the lens of evolving eyes, but an unchanging heart. I hope you enjoy the journey just as much as Dad and I have. Victor D. Rodgers Jr.

FATHERHOOD

"The state of being a father." This is the definition of fatherhood that I found while researching the word. What makes a man need to study the word fatherhood? I would much rather discuss the man behind the word. Fatherhood states that it begins the moment a child is born. I found that remarkably interesting. I had to think about this definition; Does a man simply become a father as soon as a child is born? Is there a difference between a Daddy and a father? Deep! Nah, but we know there are a whole lot of daddies that can fit that perspective. I summarized the definition as simply one's father; but does that word really encompass fatherhood? To me, fatherhood was deeper than a baby being born. It was more than the moment of conception. Hindsight was not 20/20. After some self-reflection, I knew that this journey was not for the faint-hearted, not to be treated like the Indy 500, and not for those too fragile of the mind. While I fell down a research rabbit hole, I found another definition of father that said, "a man in relation to his child." I believe, personally, that his child could be updated to "A" child, but that is another conversation. I homed in on a certain phrase in the definition, "in relation." For anything or anyone to be in relation, they must have some type of connection. This takes the time, the ultimate currency, and sacrifice that you endure in fatherhood. To be in a relationship also means to always stay aboard the ship even if it's sinking, even if the co-captain is unable to assist, you stay on the ship. This is that father's relationship with his family and children, is not just a title but an active connection; by blood but also love and understanding. A keen sense of propinquity. My babies call me daddy, go figure, but the overarching title, father, is what I embodied. Do we enter fatherhood automatically, or is this a title specifically reserved for those who embark on that journey? The actual time, effort, and sacrifice that accompanies fatherhood.

I feel like I have been on a forever hands-on training course in my fatherhood journey; full of ups, downs, twists, turns, successes, and failures, all of which have molded me into a better father and man. Through adverse situations that I swear appear out of thin air or even a wrong turn I may have made my way back where. I am forever learning to be malleable because my relationship with my kids is fluid. Marriage is fluid, and family is filled with personalities, and needs, and wants a father to do everything in his power to cater to them. Kids are changing, learning, and growing and deserve some understanding and empathy from a father. Even when I am short on energy and patience and may lose both, I'm writing this to say this I love this journey and I'm sure I can't be the only brotha who feels like damn, this what I'm made for. I am writing this not as a manual nor as a self-help information. It is more-so a therapy session with myself because I have not written any music in a while, that's my passion. So, with the main inspiration being a suggestion from my Momma a few years ago, I decided to write about my role as a father and how I manage this role. In the words of the great Jay Hova, "just my thoughts, just what I was feelin' at the time" I had to spill through a novel instead over a mic. Hopefully, these lines can find their way into the lives of those who read them and move them in any way that they see fit.

I became a father four times over in a truly short amount of time. I had my first child Dec. 2016, number 2 Dec. 2018, number 3 Feb. 2020, and number 4 Jan. 2021. At this moment I have a 6-year-old, 4-year-old, 3-year-old, and a 2-year-old and these are the seven jewels if you will, that I carry while raising my wife and I children as I travel along my journey of fatherhood. I call them jewels because they gave me a little shine of my own. These gems I uncovered, some innately, others as the journey went on, helped shape how I work as a man and father. The glow in some form of fashion through the effort I give to be a father. Yes, it also takes work, don't let anybody tell you differently. They help me work at maximum ability even when my tank is running on fumes. Through various stories and situations, I will explain how these jewels have contributed to my fatherhood journey. They are Communication, Consistency, Discipline, Patience, Prayer, Sacrifice, Adaptability, and in the end.... Purpose.

COMMUNICATION – LISTENING AND UNDERSTANDING FOR THE CONNECTION

Dad was new to all of what was taking place. He had three girls and 1 boy. A 7-year-old, a 5-year-old, and 4-year-old, and a 3-year-old. He and Mom would have many conversations regarding how to interact with the children as a whole and each one individually.

"Girls are different honey," Mom would tell Dad.

"I'm sure they are," Dad would respond.

Dad would be faced with this dilemma many times over the years but there was one situation involving his 4-year-old Marie Lynn. Potty training Marie Lynn was a lot more difficult, and frustrating, and needed a lot more patience and A LOT more communication. Marie Lynn was more emotional, and words and tone mattered a lot. Dad and Mom could with a stern voice say, "OK Reign, if you use the bathroom on yourself, it's going to be a problem." Reign, after a couple of mistakes, understood what this meant very well. Marie Lynn on the other hand did not respond efficiently to stern voices and tones. Tears and confusion filled her mind and face. She did not respond to loud voices, or even "OK Marie Lynn, if you use the bathroom on yourself, it's going to be a problem." Obviously because right after that she had an accident watching TV. She cried and cried. Dad had to go back to the drawing board. He suggested to Mom that they try more of a reward approach instead of a more disciplinary approach. They sat Marie Lynn down and explained to her that whenever she went to the potty, she would receive a reward, a prize, BUT they did not let her know what the prize was; they just emphasized the prize with their tone and the way they communicated. They mentioned that the prize could be candy, another snack, or even more screen time. Marie Lynn's eyes lit up. After a couple of mistakes, Marie Lynn called out to Dad, "Daddy, Daddy, I gotta go potty." While she was using the bathroom, Mom and Dad praised her nonstop and showered her with words of love and encouragement, and when she was done, Dad pulled Marie Lynn's tablet from behind his back. "Good job baby girl, you have just earned 15 minutes of screen time." Her eyes lit up with excitement and she reached out to grab it.

"Whoa, we can't forget to wipe and wash our hands first." Marie Lynn chuckled with embarrassment. Mom taught her how to wipe, that's gonna take some work. She washed her hands and Dad gave her the tablet.

"Thank you!" Marie Lynn said.

"You're welcome baby girl, now remember where do we go to use the bathroom?" Dad asked her.

"THE POTTY!" she shouted with excitement. From that day forth it never took any type of stern communication or a disciplinary type of tone for Marie Lynn. Dad was learning that she was a lot more emotional and internalized communication differently than his oldest daughter. As time passed Dad began to understand how to communicate with each of his children differently. He learned that even though they were small children, listening was just as important as talking. Each child would communicate in their own way how they were feeling. Reign was more outgoing with her feelings and expressed them vocally, but she opened more to Mom than Dad. Marie Lynn was more vocal in expressing her opinion when asked to do certain things and would ask "Why?" Dad began to learn that both of his oldest girls would question "Why?" You would think because Dad grew up with a brother, it would be very easy to communicate with Prince, of course, there is some truth to that, but he also was learning that Prince too was different, and he would have to learn as he got older the different ways to communicate with him also. Prince was still learning that hearing "No" was not the end of the world and Dad knew he would constantly have to teach him through effective but not hostile communication. Being patient, and consistent would show Prince discipline, even if he did not know what it was yet. Dad knew that Prince was always watching. Dad discovered every day the power of effective communication, being present and supportive with your words but stern when needed and being an active listener.

Consistency and communication can go hand in hand and at the end of the day, how you say, what you say, and when you say matters. It is relevant to strangers and family members and in Fatherhood. I would try and communicate with my kids as early as when they were in the womb. Through music, singing, talking, mini convos.........Good times. My oldest would get to moving in the womb when she heard Outstanding by The Gap Band. My 4-year-old, I have a video of her bouncing at 2 years old, right when the beat dropped listening to SiR's - Let My Hair Down. It is all communication especially when they see you smile and then they smile.

I had to learn to communicate differently with each of my four children. Each has their way of dealing with emotions and being stern or not stern. I gave an example of my 3-year-old son in consistency concerning the hug to soothe him when he is crying to express himself. A simple hug communicated to him that everything was ok, and he could be calm and not anxious. My oldest would cease to function if she were doing something wrong and gave her a look. My youngest, the 2-year-old girl, I must say you have to be a little stern with her. She runs on a "let me see what you're gonna do about it first" type of time. So far, I would say she has the most run-ins with the rod not being spared. My wife and I were astonished to learn she was more bout it than my 4-year-old at her age. She has grown up to receive a sweeter, more patient approach. Ultra-sensitive so any ounce of being stern will cause further frustration for her and impatience to finish simple tasks. I try and speak to her as calmly as I can even in moments of my own frustration. May even aid in what she is frustrated with instead of trusting her to move passed the vexation. That is a gift and curse because I want her to figure it out. Overall, communication has taught me to be patient by listening to understand and appreciate.

Communication in fatherhood taught me how to be more aware of how people may be feeling and how to address it appropriately because, in fatherhood, your kids can all be feeling totally different feelings all at the same time, each with his/her own solution that won't just be a temporary fix but a hours long dose of communication. I gave examples of verbal and nonverbal, each form just as effective. Communication in fatherhood helped me to understand what I feed my children mentally and verbally can affect their communication for life in some instances. The music I play, what they watch, and how my wife and I communicate may be the most important so Fatherhood at length is family. And family communication should be the first resort and last resort, whatever is in between those stays should be arbitration. In Fatherhood, a man who can communicate is rich without shine.

CONSISTENCY – RELIABLE FRAMEWORK

Dad and Mom were both hardworking, loving, and dedicated to their children. As their family grew from Reign, Marie Lynn, to Prince, and finally Nicole, Dad knew that it was important to be consistent with their love and dedication. He knew that this consistency would shape his kid's future and help them with self-discipline and self-control. Consistency could build family traditions, accountability, and responsibility through actions and results. Mom and Dad were asked on many occasions "Man how do you get your kids to go to bed at 8p every night without any fuss?"

"Consistency," Dad would say. You must be consistent and show kids routine and stick to it even when kids may fight back or not want to adhere to routine. "They will appreciate it and you definitely will appreciate it," he would tell those who asked.

It would come to a point where at nighttime the kids would remind Dad himself, "Daddy, Daddy we gotta take a bath," Reign would remind the entire house. Every night Mom and Dad would pray with the kids; through this example, this routine would bear fruit. It was that consistency that instilled a want to pray in our children. When it's time to pray they often argue about who is saying the prayer.

"Ok, time to say our prayers," Dad said.

"My turn!" shouted Reign, "No me!" said Marie Lynn, "I wanna do it," said Prince, "Me too," it was Nicole bringing up the rear.

"Ok, Marie Lynn, your turn, Reign you prayed last night," Dad instructed.

"Awww," the rest of the kids said in unison.

Mom and Dad did not even have to guide Marie Lynn on what to say or do for she had heard so many nights in a row Mom and Dad pray and what they said. She was able to formulate her own prayer in her own way, in her own childlike point of view. That night while lying in bed after they had said their nightly prayers, Dad looked at Mom. "Man, it is so dope how the consistency in our routines and values has made an impact on the kids. They know what to expect, and it is helping them grow in their own way and find their own voice." Mom smiled and told Dad how much she loved the direction they were going, she said that it was reassuring to see that they have a clear understanding of what is expected, and it is beautiful how through our examples they continue to grow and develop as individuals.

In the evening, the kids learned that dinner was a family affair and that everyone eats dinner together. If Dad or Mom were working late the first thing they would say, "We gotta wait for Mommy, or we gotta wait for Daddy." These routines and values were important for Dad as a father. He wanted the kids to understand the importance of fellowshipping and breaking bread together as a family every day. Dad was such a presence in the home each day, the children felt this consistency, this built habits, traditions, and memories. Dad and his family started a tradition of family movie night every Tuesday no matter what. This was a promise that Dad was determined to keep, and it reinforced the value of family that he wanted to instill in his kids. As they say, we all we got, we all we need, and he hoped the consistency that he and Mom would show from here on out would build confidence and security in the children for years to come.

I have found that to execute, to stay on top, to progress even further; it requires consistency. Consistency, honestly in my opinion, is high on the list of reasons why people don't achieve their goals. We usually go full head of steam, sometimes without a true, concrete plan without contingencies. Then when things get a little out of your control you slow down and eventually come to a complete stop. That is what it looks like to kill consistency. Now, how do you address consistency in fatherhood?

Someone told me it takes 21 days to build a habit. I know myself so I would have to double that. When it came to fatherhood, consistency has made my life and my family's life as easy as you can with a home of six, stair-steppers included. For the last 6 years while working from home, I have had 1 of my kids at home with me for the first year of their life. I have had 2 at home for a short period of time. People asked me how I have kept and achieved, even in a world where chaos is beautiful, but balance is forever. Routine and consistency.

Both work hand in hand and allow for smooth operations for even the basics of parental responsibilities like setting a bedtime and sticking with it. My kids love routine. Of course, some nights they fuss but that's where consistency kicks in. On the journey of fatherhood, I have discovered that you also need time for yourself as a man. Routine and Consistency help carve out much-needed time for yourself. You can set a time for yourself; this routine and consistency create healthy boundaries that you must respect.

I also noticed that I had to be consistent in the way I raised my kids and communicated with my kids. Kids will point out hypocrisy even if they do not know what the word means. They call out inconsistencies, I know mine do. For my 3-year-old son, if he is fussy, or crying trying to express himself, a simple hug would consistently soothe him to the point he would expect it and if he didn't have it, the situation is critical at that point. This simple gesture, a consistent hug, was like medicine with no side effects.

My oldest girl never forgets promises or plans. She yearns for my consistency when it comes to making decisions, this includes discipline also. I try to stay calm, cool, silly Dad even in discipline so now I have noticed I can 95% of the time give her a look and that solves the issue. It is just so important to build routines and be a consistent man in fatherhood. A wise lady, my grandmother once said, "don't start nothing you can't finish."

DISCIPLINE – CONQUERING GOALS AND GUIDING WITH LOVE

Aw hell, Dad thought to himself. It was Jan 2020; Dad had just received his program plan for his BA in Cyber Security. For years he had been writing music, although particularly good, he kept it real to himself about a week after he had found out he and Mom were having their 3rd child; even more exciting was the first boy! Dad must have looked like Tiger Woods after sinking the putt to win the Masters. You would have thought Mom had scored the winning touchdown. They could not be happier. But as a man, that celebration turned into a heightened awareness. Yes, after each kid Dad had felt this, but this was more than that. This was conviction. Dad thought to himself, *God I feel like I am goin nowhere fast, I need a solution, if*

I gotta give up this music. I am not willing to do it, but I will because it is your will. Give me a sign, Amen.

It was a normal day, working from home. Mom had left for the day, she a had full day of clients. Reign was at daycare and Marie Lynn was home with Dad. She was about 2 months old. Dad was still trying to figure out his ultimate move for his family. That was his why, the why that he knew was attached to his soul. While going through work emails, he noticed one that said Supervisor certification training. Dad really did not think much of it when he saw it, started to scroll past it, but something about the sender made him want to open the email and see what it was about. It was from his old supervisor who had been hired for the position he was currently in. She had moved on to another department. The training was free, and it was at a community college nearby. Dad had already taken his fair of college hours that he should have graduated twice. He knew his ultimate downfall had been discipline. He had not felt the pressure to really stay a steady course through anything adverse but continued to persevere and finish it up. *I guess this is a sign.* Dad thought. It did not take long until Dad was enrolled and beginning to start school. Something he hadn't. done in what, half a decade? Although he was in school, he still had not fully made the decision to put the music to the side for an extended period. Dad was that committed, and it was commendable but again he wrestled with discipline in that part of his life as well because he wanted to be there for his family. Discipline would have solved both dilemmas. Dad was enrolled in this certification program for one year. The multitasking of working from home and taking care of the child required the discipline that Dad would need to complete this training and that he did. He would study during whatever downtime he had during the day when it was only him and Marie Lynn. She was still in that phase of sleeping much of the day which provided some study time to complete tasks. Dad would also use any downtime on the weekend to complete assignments. It took about 6 months of this discipline for Dad to complete that training. Little did he know this was 1 of 2 signs. During a lull of workday, Dad had a sudden inkling to just search for tuition reimbursement on his company's website. He found that they not only did reimbursement, but they were offering to pay for tuition for school for certain programs at a select number of schools. *God, this is another sign.* Dad thought. After hours of searching and narrowing down majors, Dad decided to go with a BA in Cybersecurity. This was a major step for him.

He had made the decision to put his music aspirations on the back burner and take a more practical approach to providing for his family. He felt going back to school could provide a more secure future for his children, but he wanted to choose an industry that was forever growing with a very lucrative earning potential. He chose tech and eventually cyber security. After being years removed from his last attempt at reaching a college degree Dad knew it was one thing that kept him from achieving. It was not that he wasn't smart enough couldn't understand the material, or that it was too hard. It was discipline. It was on those nights when Dad knew he should be studying, he would tell himself I will *get to it tomorrow,* knowing damn well he wouldn't. It was those moments back in college 15 years ago when there was a party going on and a big test the next day, Dad would tell himself, *Ehh, I know enough, it is not that hard, I'll pass,* yeah....... FAIL. It was those nights when he knew he should be burning the midnight oil to gain more knowledge, he would tell himself, *let me get a couple more episodes of this show, I will get to the studies,* and next thing you know, SLEEP. It was discipline that could hold a man back from his purpose and destiny and although it took Dad years, I mean years, to understand this he was determined to earn this degree. I put my pride and ego aside, I was focused on creating a better life for my family. I spoke with God. I weighed the time I would have to relinquish trying to make a name in the music industry versus the practicality of going to school and majoring in a lucrative career that could provide more security for my family. I ended up focusing on tech, specifically Cyber Security. This was the start of 2020 right before the COVID-19 pandemic. We were three kids in, a 3-year-old, a 1-year-old, and my son who was born right before COVID. We had just started renting a house for more space, the irony. My wife was exhausted. I was starting school looking to earn my way into a new career and working from home, usually with a child being a heavenly distraction. It took a lot of discipline for me to study every night after loving my kids, giving time to my job, and giving energy to my wife. The irony is when I was in college with truly little responsibilities and an ample amount of time, I was sorely lacking in the discipline department. Now when things were harder something in me clicked. I found a silver lining during the COVID-19 pandemic. We were at home for so long and minimized our outside adventures even when the numbers started to go down; I was able to make the most of that time to build some consistency and a routine. Discipline is the catalyst for consistency. If you cannot find the discipline to sacrifice for what you want, I am sure there is someone else who needs it more than you. As the program started in January, Dad made it a point to have a schedule on how to be efficient but not burn himself out doing too much.

He would complete his readings Monday and Tuesday night before bed no matter what. Wednesday he would take a break and spend some time with his family and wife. Thursday he would complete actual work, quizzes, activities, etc. Friday and Saturday he would use as days to just supplement anything if he had time and Sunday, he would make sure everything was finished and complete any tests. This was a level up from the level of discipline it took for him to complete the supervisor certification. The key was being disciplined and to maintain self-control and adhere to the standard that he had set forth. Even when you really want to pivot from that standard it is important to abstain from distractions and even self-doubt, endure to reach that goal of earning that degree. The first couple of months were easy going well, Dad had functioned at that standard that was set, and he was passing classes with flying colors, not to mention there was a worldwide pandemic that truthfully made it easier to stay home and stick to the plan. As the months passed Dad discovered that he had to face his nemesis, College Algebra. A class he had failed to pass since his first year at the University of North Texas. He knew that in the past challenging circumstances were detrimental to carrying on discipline and it was easy to drift away and next thing you know, you are still at square one trying to complete your goals. This college algebra class started off just like it did his first year; frustration, doubt, and wanting to go another route because it was "hard" started to set in. Dad took a step back, prayed by himself, prayed with Mom, and with some stern encouragement and motivation from Mom, he adapted his standard to study more and take extra steps to ensure he understood the material. At the end of the month, Dad earned a B in that college algebra course. Through discipline, Dad completed his program and in April 2022 he was in New Hampshire at this commencement with Mom and sister-in-law receiving his Bachelor of Science in Cyber Security. Through discipline Dad had made the Dean's list 1 out of 2 years and finished with his highest GPA, 3.3, he had ever had at any moment in college some 10-15 years earlier. Through rigorous intent and organization, Dad had mastered discipline in this endeavor. He understood that for him it was a constant battle, and he would master it at every turn with every goal he wanted to complete.

I can say a lot about discipline because it is the jewel that I spend the most time forging while praying for a lender's hand because it's also a gem that I struggle to carry. I want to be vulnerable here and I yield. Even when I win, there is some meat left on the bone and with discipline, I would have been fulfilled. Discipline can manifest unhealthy habits or good habits. For me it was not about creating new unhealthy habits; I am who I am. I was already praying and working on unloading unpleasant habits. It was about creating good new habits that would push me to the point of being so uncomfortable, I would transform into another form of myself. This new shape could fit any problem with a solution and as a father, I discovered that every day you would, could, and should be solving problems. Through discipline, I could shed the weight of procrastination that would sometimes limit my efficiency. I was less productive than I knew I could be but just enough to not alarm me.

I also found discipline in fatherhood. Or rather discipline was kicking my ass in these current rounds and fatherhood forced me to admit it. One lesson, that may seem insignificant and simple for some, I had to learn to wake up every day earlier than a night owl would appreciate; The night is when I can think, it is quiet, it is still, I can create, I could live in the night. It was Me time, iTime; I have an amazing wife so now it is WE time. So, I enjoyed the night, and it was hard to just turn off my brain and just go to sleep. This was during the baby phase, then daycare, and now it is school and daycare. I soon discovered this was every day. Really negro? When you work from home you get used to waking up only having to worry about making sure you are on time. And even then, for me as I was getting burnt out in my position at work, logging in could mean rolling over punching in a few words, and rolling back over if I felt like it. Usually, I was up, but that was my choice. I was disciplined in that I knew what time to wake up for my job. Now I was beginning a new level of discipline. It was not one, not 2, not 3, not 4, but 5 people including myself who I was responsible for waking up early and on time. This was amplified on Sundays. I'd like to thank my uncle for those words about being the head of the house and getting your family ready for church.

"You know when you stayed with me, I would have y'all upright, right," my uncle said in a gentle, authoritarian tone.

"Yea, you're right," I replied.

"Alright then don't make me have to hurt you now," he said.

It was the trivial things you must master first to even get the disc in discipline. Sounds simple but it is usually the simple things which build up and knock us off our path.

Of course, disciplining children is a part of the journey, and I will spare the rod if a rod needs to be spared. On the rare occasion that event needs a rod then we have no spare. We are rollin' on. Now, we got that out of the way. I am still learning to understand that each of my kids may require distinct levels of discipline. The oldest understands a simple look but she likes to negotiate. Sometimes she listens, and sometimes she must understand what I said the first time will be the same as the last time. Disciplining children requires you to be consistent. Being consistent in not only correcting but also showing my kids the correction in a controlled, non-emotional way. If my child uses a curse word, I cannot laugh that one time then try and discipline the next time and let that turn into a pattern. They are confused at that point. I learned to react in a disciplinary fashion the first time an incident occurs by explaining what they did wrong and correcting them. Giving my children reasons to make good choices was also a part of discipline. They began to learn that if we cleaned our room consistently without Mommy or Daddy having to instruct us to do so could lead to rewards, more screen time, snacks, treats, etc. I was able to practice discipline also by providing consistent routine for my children. Sticking to my guns. I would discuss with other parents about their children's habits daily and most of them would marvel at how I would allow no screen time on our YouTube throughout the week or at dinnertime. Monday, Wednesday, and Thursday we read books before bedtime, there was no iPad or video games Monday-Thursday. No YouTube watching during the week. Tuesdays were family movie nights. Fridays and weekends were free for all. You can play your video games and iPad; watch YouTube ONLY after you clean your room and aid Mom and Dad with house duties. Other parents would complement my wife and me on the discipline it took to stay consistent with this routine, and they would even tell us that they would like to try this approach in parenting. I believe this discipline and routine will go a long way in shaping my children's future. They will understand delayed gratification through discipline. They will be more prepared to pursue challenging careers that require discipline; they will be prepared and understand that chasing your dreams requires discipline. I practice discipline in my life as a man and as a father. Without it, I could not have made it this far and this gem is one that I continue to work on and sometimes struggle with to this day.

PATIENCE – GROWTH AND UNDERSTANDING

It was going to be one of those days.... Dad could tell as soon as he woke up the kids for school. He had to ask Reign not one, not 2, not 3, but 4 times to get out of bed to come to the table for breakfast. She eventually moved, but her face said it all. She was tired and annoyed. Marie Lynn appeared from the bathroom with lips poked out, mad that she had to wake up. She walked to the table for breakfast and mistakenly walked into a wall, pouting, with her head down. Dad tried not to laugh but being a father, you notice that when kids pout or are unnecessarily angry about something or go out of their way to have an attitude, they usually hurt themselves; just one of the many observations that Dad had made as a father. Prince was over the morning as soon as he woke up, from whiny to annoyed at anything around him, he had a stern face all the way to the breakfast table. Nicole woke up slowly and walked to the table, with a sharp tongue she said,

"Mawie stop lookin at me!"

Nicole had a 6 am attitude with an 11 pm level of disrespect in her voice. Marie Lynn just stared back at her; lips still poked out like she was mad at a dream. Dad didn't have to try and diagnose the situation, he knew they tried desperately to stay up last night, holding on to that little bit of playtime, even after Mom and Dad had said go to bed so much, they should have been seeing that phrase in their dreams. Dad had to check himself in this predicament because he understood too many times that when the kids were in this mode, his patience would be tested tenfold. But he knew not to let their antics affect his day, practicing patience was the key. Dad had been trying to keep his patience intact even though he was too putting in late nights and earlier mornings to take the next level in his life and secure a better future for his family, something that would take patience. Dad knew with everything going on it was easy to lose patience with the kids, but he thought, not today, Satan.

"So, what have we learned this morning?" Dad said. There was silence.

"Sandman got your tongue?"

"This is why Mommy and Daddy stress to you beautiful babies why it's important to get some sleep at night, especially when we have to wake up early for school, right Reign?"

"Yeaaa…," she said softly, still tired.

"Prince?" Dad asked, "You understand why you have to go to bed at night, so you won't be tired?"

"Yes," he said, still annoyed.

"Marie Lynn, Nicole, y'all got it?" Nicole was the stubborn one.

"Yea, I'm tiyurd" said Marie Lynn, with exhaustion written all over her face.

"I know," Dad replied.

"Ms. Nicole, you understand?"

She tried to cry, "Uh uh, you are ok, you understand that you have to go to bed at nighttime for school?" Dad asked her again.

"Yes," she said through her sniffles.

"Ok, anybody needs a morning hug?"

In unison they all said some variation of me, I do. Dad and Mom gave them each a hug. Mom had breakfast locked and loaded on the table fruit, yogurt, eggs. A slice of bacon for Dad's fellow swine eater, Marie Lynn. And a silver dollar pancake. The true test was getting them all out the door on time while they were in this state of exhaustion. That required even more patience. They also, as kids do, became a lot whinier, frustrated, inability to complete simple tasks (that always baffled Dad) all due to exhaustion.

"Marie Lynn, baby girl, take your time and put your pants on."

"Reign, why are you back in bed, go get dressed, you know you don't like being late."

"Prince, nope, I said no paw patrol shoes, you have a nice outfit on man, go get some more shoes." He tried sadly walking away, shoulders slumped.

"Hey, straighten up, head up. We don't walk around like that," Dad said to him while he walked away.

"Nicole, can you go get yourself a pull-up, Dad asked" She started to cry. Mom gave her another hug, consoled her, and got them dressed, while Dad fixed lunches and got backpacks together. Mom and Dad both were praying for more patience with their children. This morning was one of many examples of why they needed to ask God for more patience. Dad was learning that having 4 children, every day your patience could be tested in 4 different ways at any given time. It was difficult sometimes to navigate and honestly, Dad would lose his patience sometimes, but he tried his hardest to apologize to his children if he knew he lost his patience for a very minute occurrence.

"Ok, everybody to the door!" They all of course took their sweet time walking to the door. Dad didn't mind they had about 10 minutes to spare, and school was across the street.

"Daddy," said Prince, "Can I get my car?"

"Bam, The'e it iz!" Dad shouted. Prince tried not to smile but he couldn't help it. Mom and Dad got the kids in the car quicker than a NASCAR pitstop and that's exactly what it looked like with 4 toddlers. When they arrived in the parking lot of the school. Dad's patience was stretched even further by the bus cutting it close.

"That paper said 7:30 right?" Dad asked Mom in a sarcastic tone. She tried not to chuckle.

"Yea I believe it did," she said.

"Oh ok," said Dad. Time went by, 7:30....7:40....7:43.

"Mannnn we gotta get gone, they are taking forever.... Prince go back to ya sea-... Nicole stop all that cryin, Rei-, I mean Marie Lynn stop standing on the armrest, what's wrong with you! Reign can we hold off the questions, I'm trying to see where Marie Lynn's bus is at, man where this bus is!"

"Be patient Daddy!" Prince said. Reign and Marie Lynn both begin to snicker. Dad looked at Mom with a look of, *really?* Mom smiled a big smile, "Yea, patience Daddy," she said.

The Bible says that love is patience, patience is love, and love doesn't rejoice in wrongdoing but rejoices in truth. That resonates deeply for I have found myself impatient in Fatherhood. I guess at times I couldn't fully process the perspective of my children. I've had to take a step away and maybe take a sec in another room when my kids were babies, and they were going through it. That second allowed me to regroup and collect my thoughts and how I wanted to manage a situation that was becoming overwhelming. You realize how easy it is to be quick to anger, the opposite of what the Bible says, but it's easier to take that route of impatience and anger because it is a temporary fix for a lot of circumstances. I have now proven patience as a strength of mine, I've embraced that challenge of being cool, calm, and collected even when my kids are chaotic, cruel, and cunning. Exercising patience usually uncovers a solution that is long-term or one that you can use again under similar conditions. It's as simple as when getting my baby boy dressed and we are running late, he still desperately wants to show me he can take off his own shirt. I know he is just trying to practice independence but I'm like *deep sigh* Baby boy we are running late but his face afterward and the genuine joy he has, without patience, I'm sure I would have said No, and another NO more sternly, let me do it. I've also had to be real with myself for I am an adult and if I would manage my time more wisely, perhaps he would have time to show me his independence and I would naturally be more patient. This is an underlying root of some of my patience flaws. I've learned that practicing patience can be essential to my children's ability to be independent. The more patient I am with them in completing simple tasks, the more they feel emboldened and confident to complete those tasks on their own. This can lead to them undertaking more challenging tasks that they would normally look for Mommy and Daddy to complete. I had to be patient with my kids when it came to them learning how to brush their teeth properly, instead of always stepping in. I had to be patient when my kids were learning how to clean up after themselves after dinner, they would forget because they were so used to Mommy and Daddy cleaning up the table after them. Eventually, they began to do it without even having to ask. I didn't have to yell or get frustrated or say "Never mind I'll do it" I stayed consistent and patient. It took the ultimate patience when sleep training. The wife and I were determined as parents to not let our kids get in the habit of sleeping in our bed at bedtime. It took a lot of patience to get through the whining, crying, separation anxiety and not giving in. Being consistent and creating boundaries, yes, boundaries for babies, infants, toddlers, and kids are important. I would hear often parents say how do you deal with the crying and constantly ask, "Can we sleep with you?" It was the consistency of my wife and I explaining to the kids that you have your own room and bed for a reason. Comforting them without them sleeping with us by reading, lo-fi music, whatever it would take within the realm of sanity to be consistent. It was well worth it. I had to learn to be an example of patience as a father to my children by not losing patience when they would consistently not listen or do something wrong. Regulating my emotions in times of distress is crucial in practicing patience and being an example of patience to my children. Discovering triggers that would cause me to lose patience and planning for those triggers is a great strategy. For example, if I knew that my kids took longer to get ready in the morning than I could appreciate, I started to lay their clothes out the night before and make lunch the night before, which made the morning commute to school a lot easier, even though I would be sacrificing my me time at night that I enjoyed. I believe another strategy I used for teaching patience that was created by having multiple children is teaching them about taking turns. We had 4 kids sharing one bathroom, so patience was a must. Teaching them that not everything was a race or competition and that completing tasks the right way the first time required patience.

Potty training is probably the ultimate tester of patience. Add the fact I was a father of 4, so that meant 4 different avenues to arrive at the same goal. I had a lot of help with my oldest daughter. It was simple. A lot more attention could be devoted to teaching just her. She also was around family who took the time to help keep her on schedule and consistent, there is that word again, consistency; we will get back to that. I was still working from home, so it provided a clearer road to the potty. My 2nd oldest was the one that required a lot more patience and nurturing. It wasn't that she didn't know what the potty was, she just would decide that whatever else she was doing was more important than going to use the bathroom, until the last minute. Then she was even more stubborn to go when you knew that she had to go, she did the typical bathroom ballet, a dance around the fact she needed to go potty. I am sure a couple of times I lost my patience, and I would appreciate it even more with my son. I recognized my growth by being patient. We let him grow into his own time to get ready to use the bathroom. It wasn't a lot of routine involved or building a schedule. I would speak about using the potty regularly and show him what it was when I would go. He would eventually get curious and want to go. That was a part of the patience. In my patience, I had found a solution that I did not have in the past. I grew into this solution, being real with myself and allowing for change. I guess I was blessed with my youngest daughter. She was the easiest to potty train. All the patience I had lost was replaced by patience that was fortified and evolving, proactively recognizing a better solution before you lose tolerance. Upon some self-reflection I wanted my 2nd daughter to be potty trained quicker because we ultimately would save some money on diapers. I noticed it was selfish because my daughter was learning these basic human self-care actions. Patience told me that if I genuinely loved her, I would let her take her time. Patience, that's love.

CHAPTER

7

PRAYER – SPIRITUAL ANCHOR

Bong.... Bong.... Bong "Excuse me teachers please release the car riders for dismissal" It was a muggy spring evening, and the sound of kids exiting school began to swell. Dad stood outside the school among the cars and parents or guardians who were waiting to pick up their kids. Dad held a sign that read Reign, his daughter's name, alerting the teachers that he was there to pick her up. Smiling 1st-grade faces began to exit the building, teachers calling the names of children based on the signs they saw; some kids walked, some ran, but all were ecstatic as they embraced their loved ones. "Daddy, daddy!" shouted Reign. Reign walked with a purpose toward Dad, and he knew something was on her mind.

"Reign, Reign!" Dad shouted back, "How was school?"

"School was good................. Is it going to rain?" Reign asked. Dad looked at the sky, there were a few clouds, some grey, but in the distance, he could see several big, bold, dark clouds moving in. Dad knew that Reign, his oldest daughter, was ter-rified of thunderstorms.

"Ehh not right now but it might, hopefully just rain though, right?" The look on Reign's face was concerned but Dad could tell she was trying to keep it together.

"Yea", she said softly, holding her hands to her mouth as she twiddled her fingers nervously. They walked back to the car and Dad noticed Reign was fixated on the clouds and the sky. As they got in the car to wait for Marie Lynn's bus to arrive, Reign asked again as she stared out of the car window with a look of nervousness "Daddy, are you sure it's not gonna rain?"

"No, I can't be sure baby girl, only God knows, and time will tell" Dad was low-key amazed because he too could sense some rain coming and it seemed that whenever Reign would ask about rain, sure enough, it rained but he also didn't want to alarm her anymore. At the age of 6 she was becoming some-what of a weather whisperer. As they sat in the parking lot of the school waiting on Dad's 2nd oldest girl Marie Lynn, Reign told Dad about her day and learning about addition and being a good citizen and even a little 1st grade drama.

"Yep, and so and so didn't want me to play with him be-cause I think she thinks he likes me, she's just' being a hater right Daddy?"

Dad tried not to laugh, with a smile "Yep baby girl she is a true hater." Dad and Reign dusted off their shoulders. "UH, but he is ya' friend, that's a boy remember that" Dad was low-key doing a little fatherhood hatin', but he had to let it be known. He could hear Mom in his ear, that's her boyfriend, Yea, ight. A few minutes later Marie Lynn's bus arrived, and she was her usual bubbly, carefree self. "Hi Daddy, I played games today, and I told a bully that his momma stank since he told me that I stank." She had a sly smirk on her face, with a hint of 'well you told me to say it.'

"Did you tell the teacher first, Dad said?"

"Yep, but he said it again."

"Well, I'm glad you stood up for yourself, we don't start it, but you protect yo' peace" Dad gave Marie Lynn a high 5, strapped them both in their car seat, and was about to head home when he heard, "Can we hear trolls!"

As Dad and the girls were pulling up to the house, Mom had pulled up at the same time after picking up the other 2 munchkins in the family, a 3-year-old, only boy, Prince and 2-year-old baby of the family Nicole. "Mommy, Daddy!" Shouted all the kids as they opened the car doors. Hugs all around.

"Hey babies, ok let's get in the house, take ya shoes off, put them in your closet, you got about an hour of tv time before dinner," said Mom.

Dad threw back his head and yelled "Taco Tuessssssd-ddaaay!!!!!"

A resounding "yayyyy!!" filled the house as the kids did what mom asked and ran to the tv. Mom cooked and made plates, a quick Taco Tuesday meal; Dad went outside to bring in trash cans, he could see that the dark ominous clouds that were in the distance were gradually rolling in. Oh, Lawd he thought, Reign gonna have a fit. No sooner than he walked back in the house he could hear Reign ask from the dinner table "Mommy is it gonna rain?"

Mom paused for a moment and looked outside, "It might, looks like it huh?"

"Oh man," Reign said. Her eyebrows raised, she slowly put her right hand over her mouth, worried. "It's Rainin' Daddy?" Prince asked.

"Not right now my guy" Dad tried his best to keep the nerves of Reign settled. The other 3 kids really didn't care about a thunderstorm, they were gonna sleep regardless. Reign was in for a night, but I had faith she could pull through sooner than later. She could remain calm, scared but not panicked. Dinner was phenomenal.

"Thank you, mommy." Dad said. Dad had a look of a matter of fact. With a hint of thankfulness and teaching in his tone. All 4 children repeated one by one,

"Thank youuu mommy,"

"Tha' u moommy"

"Thank you, mommy,"

"Thank u mommy!" Marie Lynn shouted. As dinner was ending, it was as if the rain was the desert. Suddenly, the drizzle turned to a sprinkle, sprinkles morphed into rain, minutes later, showers. "Daddy it's raining really hard," Reign was obviously in fear. Then, BOOM, the crashing sound of thunder, BOOM, "No, no, no!" Reign jumped up with a look of terror on her face. "It's ok baby girl, let's take a bath, get our pajamas on, get ready for bed, the storm will probably pass, and we will be ok, ok?"

"Yea," said Reign in the most unsure of responses. After bath time and pajamas, Dad and Mom read a couple of books to the kids. Storytime was important, it not only was quality time for the whole family, but it reinforced those reading skills that were a major part in raising the children. It was much better than the screentime that a lot of parents told me they even allowed it at dinner time. Yea, not up in here, that was not happening with Mom and Dad.

"Ok, bedtime, let's say our prayers, everybody holds hands, close your eyes and bow your heads." Mom and Dad had been praying consistently with the children, teaching them how to pray through action. Dad made it a point to be intentional in his prayers with the children, giving them an example of how to talk to God and why it was important. As Dad instructed, the family held hands and began to pray in unison, "Now I lay me down to sleep, I pray the Lord my soul to keep, if I should die before I wake, I pray the Lord my soul to take." Dad continued "Thank you God for waking us up this morning and protecting us throughout the day. Thank you for your grace and mercy every day. Thank you for all the blessings you have bestowed on us God, even when we don't deserve it you are right on time. Thank you for protecting our children while they are away at school. Instill patience, strength, and discipline in their teachers God, and thank you for their teachers. We ask that you continue to look after our family and friends, restore their strength and faith, and heal their body, mind, and spirit. Please God bless those that sick, less, and fortunate. We ask all these blessings in Jesus' name, everybody says thank you, God."

"Thank you, God!" the kids shouted.

"Amen"

"Daddy is it still raining?" Reign asked, anxiously.

"No not right now baby girl, now go get in the bed, goodnight."

"Nite, nite," said Marie Lynn.

"Nite Daddy, Nite Mommy," said Prince.

"Ni, Ni," said Nicole.

The next morning Dad couldn't believe his ears, Boom! Boom! Thunder rolled across the gloomy morning sky. The time was around 6:15 am. It was raining cats and dogs, and the first thing Dad could think about....... Reign is gonna have a fit. As Mom and Dad started the morning routine of getting the kids ready for school the storm grew more intense. You could hear the rain hitting the windows and the wind howling as lightning lit up the sky. Dad turned on the TV to see the warnings and threats. "There is a tornado warning for the following counties.........."

"Tornado?! Daddy, Daddy it's a tornado? Where is the tornado?" Reign had heard what the weather forecaster said and immediately had questions that demanded answers.

"There is no tornado directly near us Reign." We lived in Tarrant County, and it was in Tarrant County but.... Like a father shielding his young, he tried to ease her mind by stretching the truth just a little.

"Daddy, are you sure? It's so dark outside, the wind is blowing; Look at the rain Daddy! Are you sure!?" Dad again reassured her that all would be calm shortly, that God was in control.

The next moment made every day as a father, teacher, and leader worth it. Just Priceless, a moment grandmama and granny would hit the infamous, "Hercules, Hercules, Hercules."

With fingers locked, hands up to face, head bowed, and eyes closed, Reign began praying. "God please protect us from the tornado, make it go away. Stop the rain God, protect my school, Ms. Mazi, thank you God, Amen." Reign raised her head and opened her eyes. She still had a look of uneasiness on her face, but her energy and aura gave off more of a peaceful vibration. She was practicing what had been preached to her on the power of prayer and how it could be used as a weapon of protection. Because my children always want to follow one another, the other 3 also began to pray their own unique prayer. Marie Lynn prayed for the rain to come again later that day. Prince prayed for his teacher to let him, and his friends play Mario. And Nicole just mumbled something like what Reign had prayed for.

"Than' you God, no rain, amen," said Nicole.

Dad took a quick look at Mom who gave a proud smile, he turned back to Reign, "That's how you do it, baby girl, that's all you need."

Dear God, thank you for waking me up this morning, please order my steps to make the right choices under your eyes today. Thank you for my children and my wife, thank you God for waking my family up; I ask that you protect my children while they are at school. I ask that you restore my wife's strength when she gets weary as she puts in another day's work, please restore my strength also when I get weary, in Jesus name, Amen.

It felt like a normal day, Mom and Dad woke the kids up, fed them breakfast, and made sure they were at school on time. Mom went off to work, she had several clients that day whose hair I'm sure needed some tenderness, love, and care. Dad, working from home, made himself his daily breakfast of champions after he logged into his computer for the day. He knew that today would be a challenging day. Dad thought of the meetings, after meetings, after meetings; with also the expectation of completing priority-driven tasks that could affect a company's bottom line. *So goes the life of a Security Analyst at THIS place,* he thought; a silver lining in this sarcasm was working from home and how it was perfect for the family dynamics. As he cooked his pancakes, eggs, bacon, roasted potatoes, and a side of strawberries with a glass of Treetop apple juice, not from concentrate; the sound of Kendrick Lamar's "King Kunta" resonated throughout the kitchen. For the last week that was Dad's song in the morning, followed by the playing of the whole To Pimp a Butterfly album to get the juices flowing and focus on the upcoming tasks at work. After dancing, rapping lyrics, flipping pancakes, and cleaning the kitchen while he cooked, Dad sat down at the table to enjoy this meal. "Dear God, let this meal be a nourishment for my mind, body, and soul. Thank you for the hands that prepared it and the money that paid for it. Amen"

"Ding! Ding!" went Dad's iPhone text notification. "Ding!"

Yea, they gonna have to wait, Dad thought to himself.

"Ding! Dad pivoted his attention from his meal to his phone with a little annoyance but upon noticing that it was from Mom and seeing the message preview be a little longer than usual, he knew that it had to be important. So, like any father, he had to multitask. With his fork in the right hand, he began to eat. Opening his phone with his left hand, he seen the first message from Mom.

"Babe, I don't know what to do, Ms. Smith is pretty much sayin that this is probably my last day. She knows I need this arrangement to work, I told her my plan, and we agreed to but now she is saying that I would have to pay while I am on maternity leave, or I would have to find a new location to service my clients."

"Babe, we had an arrangement," she continued. And now she is trying to break that arrangement. I knew this would happen."

Dad could hear the frustration through the messages. He could tell Mom was really going through it. Mom was pregnant and had arranged, although not in writing, to not pay any booth rent during maternity leave. She had just found this location sharing a booth with a lady who she met through family. Dad and Mom knew that this arrangement wouldn't last due to the need for Mom and Ms. Smith to have their own space. Mom was adamant about needing her own space but understood where she was, she needed to find somewhere quick to take her clients after she had just left another job that had let her go.

Dad assured Mom that this too would pass. He reminded her that over the years that they had been together, already 2 kids in with a 3rd on the way, they always bounced back. God had always shown favor.

"Calm down babe." Dad could tell she was practically yelling in the messages. "Just focus on your clients, we will get together, brainstorm our options, and come up with a solution that suits you and our family. I love you." Mom loved the message.

"Thank you, babe, I'll see you when I get home," she texted back.

Dad finished his breakfast, cleaned up what was left to clean and got back to work.

After what seemed like a longer day than usual, which could have been because while working, Dad was also thinking of solutions for his wife, and how to comfort her when she returned home. The time had come for him to pick up the kids from school and daycare.

"Hey y'all mommy has had a long day, so when she gets home, let's give her a hug and show her some love. Let her rest, ok, y'all got it?" Dad asked.

One after another the kids replied, "Yes, ok, ok. Yes."

After getting the kids situated at home. Mom texted Dad and let him know that she would be arriving later in the evening, due to a client showing up late to her appointment. Dad said it was ok just drive safe. After dinner, some tv time, baths for everyone, and a couple of stories, Dad tucked the kids into bed. Of course, they asked about Mom and if she was ok.

"Yes, Mommy is ok, she is just getting home late tonight, but I will make sure she comes in here and says goodnight to you before she goes to bed, ok?" They reluctantly said OK and Dad gave out kisses and hugs. "Goodnight, Daddy loves ya'll" he said as he went from Reign's and Marie Lynn's room to tuck them in then to Prince and Nicole's room to tuck them in. Dad then prepared Mom a hot bath, and candles, with some Miles Davis softly playing in the background. Not too many minutes later Mom walked through the door. Dad knew that Mom was already frustrated with the situation going on in the salon suite and now add to the fact that she had returned home later in the evening when the kids were in bed, he wanted to be there for her any way that he could.

"Ms. Smith said she would have to let me go and that I would have to find another suite to work out of. How can I find another suite that fast, one that I can afford? We are already stretched thin. We had an agreement and now she wants to break it. She told me that when you go on parental leave, u still must pay your house rent, right? Do people not have any empathy? She knows my situation and we talked about this several times." Mom was visibly upset bordering on the point of sadness. The frustration and annoyance were boiling over.

Dad, without saying a word, opened his arms to embrace Mom.

"We gonna be alright, I promise we will figure this out. Whatever you need me to do I will do, wherever this road takes us, we will travel together. Let me pray for you."

Dad led mom to the bedroom, they knelt together on the side of the bed and Dad began to pray.

"Dear God, we come to you humbly, with an open heart and mind we thank you for your blessings thus far. Thank you for our family and taking us safely through the day, protecting us and providing for us. Dear God, we know that trials and tribulations come and go and right now we are during a storm. I ask that you restore my wife's faith and strength. Give her a sound mind, peace of heart, and the direction that is ordered in your steps. Guide us, dear Lord, and give us more wisdom to make sound decisions that not only enrich our lives individually but that support our family. Help us to not lean on our own understanding, open our hearts and minds to hear you. I believe that you will show my wife and I the way and we will come out on the other side renewed and stronger than ever. All these blessings I ask in Jesus name, Amen."

"Amen," Mom said. "Thank you," she turned and gave Dad a kiss, then went into the bathroom where she let out a deep sigh of appreciation for the bath. The next morning Mom was up bright and early, showered, and breakfast fixed for the family. She had a smile and a look of determination on her face. After the kids were off at school, Mom told Dad that she woke up with a plan. She knew it could fail but she said she knew what she had to do. She was worried about trying to find a salon suite that fit her budget in a short amount of time, but Dad assured her that their faith would not go unnoticed. Dad gave her a kiss goodbye and went to log on for work. Around lunch time Mom came rushing through the door.

"Babe, I found a spot, I found a suite! OMG!" Mom was overwhelmed with joy.

"WHAAAATTTTT!" Dad exclaimed, sounding like Martin Lawrence from 1994. Mom laughed with joy, and they embraced and kissed like that first night conceiving Reign.

"It is even cheaper than what I was paying with Ms. Smith," she said.

"And guess what," Dad replied. "ITS YOURS!"

"I KNOW!" Mom shouted. "Ayyyeee."

"Thank you, God!" They both said at the same time. With arms stretched to the sky, Dad thought about the pain that his wife was feeling, the weariness through pregnancy.

Now I know some people will say aww that's just coincidence, it was going to happen that way. Well, I tell you what, you believe what you want to believe, but as for me and mine in this house, we worship the Lord, and my faith is unwavering. Again, the power of prayer.

This is the most valuable of the 7. Prayer. I've always been taught that prayer is the most powerful resource, entity and/or weapon, that you can use this side of heaven to get you through life. Through various teachings from those wiser than myself, I was taught the importance of instructing your children about the power of prayer also. Being intentional in making sure they understand how to pray, why we pray, and the power that manifests in your life through conversations with God. I've also learned that you not only pray when things are going bad but also when things are good, always thanking

God, through all trials and tribulations. As you can imagine there have been many twists and turns even on this short-lived, ongoing journey through fatherhood; these 7 years as a father and husband has further confirmed how powerful prayer was and is in restoring my faith, my vigor, confidence, and just my overall well-being. I've had moments where the last thing I wanted to do was pray. I was so overwhelmed with life that sometimes the enemy would have me thinking that prayer was a waste of time as if the conversations with God were not being heard. I found that wasn't the case at all but rather I would lean more so to what I thought was the correct decision; I would get caught up in manifesting how I seen the vision instead of talking to God and actively listening to his voice even when it went against how I felt my life should go. I had to understand that my walk was different and operating in the way the world said I should maneuver was contradicting to how God wanted to guide me. Even if the road was longer under God's watch, the shortcuts proved time and time again to end with the force of a crash dummy into a brick wall.

Prayer was and is incredibly significant in providing guidance, patience, and strength. Hearing my daughter pray to comfort herself amid a storm was a validation of how it could shape my children. As a father one of the greatest moments, you can appreciate is watching your kids practice what you have preached to them. Through consistency, intentionality, and a never-ending desire to instill some sense spirituality in my children, my wife and I introduced prayer at an early age to our children. My firstborn was praying on her own by the age of 3. It was confirmation that my children were sponges soaking up spiritual lessons and learning how to apply them in real life situations. She was taught how prayer was a tool in life when you need comforting, reassurance, and just the ultimate friend. My wife and I try to teach our kids that you can call on God for any and everything and while you pray, you must learn to listen to him and above all else, be patient. In teaching them about prayer we stressed patience, God was not a genie but being faithful to God and applying that faithfulness was key to unlocking God's infinite power through prayer. We incorporated prayer into our daily life by praying over our food as a family during breakfast and dinner. Currently we are instilling in them the habit of thanking God first thing in the morning when we wake them up. We incorporate prayer into our bedtime routine and give them the freedom to take turns leading the prayer every night. This teaches them to apply prayer on their own and gives them practice. It has gotten to the point even my 3-year-old wants to lead the prayer some nights. They have learned through this practice to not only pray for what they desire but most of their prayers are asking for blessings for others, asking for protection for others, asking for healing, protection and blessings for their siblings, family, and teachers. I can honestly say it has enriched their spirituality.

Some people pray for the family, specifically. I never truly prayed for a family, but I always knew I wanted to be a father even though I always thought kids were a lot. Not that they were expensive or annoying, but the responsibility of raising a human life could intimidate even the strongest among us. Welp, it turns out there is a lot and some, an abundance of joy and energy. I always knew I would be a good father. It turns out, I am. The moment I discovered I was going to be a father was the first time I said a prayer over my family. At the time my lady and I were not married. We were enthralled in a web of love, lust, youth, vigor and ambitions that would keep us in bliss all night. I remember one of the nights early in the pregnancy, my lady was sound asleep, meanwhile, my mind was racing. You would have thought the Daytona 500 was taking place in my head. Questions and worries, questions with no answers and more worries and concerns all doing laps in my brain. I had so many questions. Would he/ she be healthy? Would my lady be healthy? Would she need a C-section/natural birth? Would she survive? Would my baby be, ok? Could I provide? Yea, I'm working, 9-5, I make enough but is it enough? I have dreams, dreams of rapping my ass off for the masses but I must make time for my family, can I provide? All these questions plus countless amounts of concern all flooded my brain. I can remember looking at her so peaceful in a slumber, not understanding the fatigue and strenuous activities her body was going through but she looked oh so peaceful, an Angel carrying a miracle, life itself. At that moment, all I could do was pray. I tried to numb and suppress through weed and alcohol and yes, they did provide some relief but, in the end, what I needed was prayer. I believed that anxiousness, fear, and doubt were not of God. What I lacked was a cure, not a band-aid. What I was taught provided more than a temporary fix to problems in life and of the heart and soul. I dropped to my knees and asked God to remove any fear for that was not conducive to my faith, nor was it of him. I asked God to protect my lady, protect her body, and cover my unborn child with your cloth of protection. I asked God to protect us from all harm seen and unseen. I thanked him for this blessing he had bestowed upon us, and I thanked him for even a chance to raise a life. I thanked him for blessing me with good health to plant the seed of life. I prayed for guidance and wisdom, 2 things I still pray for to this day. Without guidance and wisdom from God, I would wander aimlessly on this journey, constantly rerouting to destinations rooted in my ego and personal desires. I asked God for patience as the head of a soon-to-be family of 6, and power only released through his faith. The power to be the man who God knew I could be as a father and head of my family. I can remember praying for a healthy baby and for my wife's health when we discovered she had pre-eclampsia and had to be admitted to the hospital immediately to begin labor. I prayed all the way home. I was on my way to go out with the fellas, and received a call from a number that I didn't know, so I ignored it. I turned up my music and kept on my way. But again, the same number called again, and left a voicemail. I checked the voicemail.

"Hi this is Dr so n so, we need you to come in, your blood pressure was higher than normal earlier at your checkup and you had protein in your urine. We need you to come in right now and pack an overnight bag. Thank you, bye." Immediately I exited and raced back to the apartment. I started praying like God please just protect them, please don't let it be anything serious. When I made it back home, still in my club clothes, I asked Mom to pack an overnight back because the Dr. had called a left a voicemail telling us to come to the hospital to-night. My wife also received the call, but it wasn't the doctor's number, the same unknown number. We started packing and sped oh so carefully to the hospital. Quickly, efficiently, and with much care, we were led to our room. I remember the nurses and the Dr., who to our unpleasant surprise was not our actual Dr. As a matter of fact, our Dr. will not be available. I felt like Seth Rogen at the end of Knocked Up. This Dr. ex-plained what the high blood pressure and protein meant, pre-eclampsia. I had no clue what the hell that was, so like I do, I hit up ol' Google. The only thing that was on my mind was the safety of mother and child.

I can remember my first birth, my wife and I (she was not my wife then) in the hospital and the magnitude of exhaustion that she was experiencing, I knew whatever level of weariness I was going through was no match. I remember going home to get more clothes and looking in the mirror at a new face, the face of a father; I looked in that mirror with so much conviction and said "God please give me strength" I had not known this foreign mixture of love, fatigue, and anxiety. I was thankful that I was able to have that moment with my daughter, holding her close. My heart close to her ear, the 2nd heartbeat heard of her fresh life. I said a small prayer for all of us, I made sure that God knew I was thankful for this moment; I knew I would need his guidance from this point on. I thanked God that mother and child were safe, alive, well, and alert. *Thank you, God,* I thought.

I prayed for forgiveness because at times I was emotionally unavailable and insensitive to my wife while she was going through what the old folks call a setback as well as being a first-time mother. I prayed that God would show me how to be a good husband when I proposed before the birth of my 2nd child in the Dominican Republic. I prayed for my wife to find some solace and security in her search for a job while praying for the 2nd child's health and well-being and still asking God for that patience and power that I would need even more with 2 kids. Prayer was there for me when my wife was dealing with medical issues, I was always praying for strength and a frame of mind that would breed positivity under circumstances that seemed dire. I had 2 daughters in and let me tell you I prayed, I prayed, Lord knows I had to pray. I still pray but now I have

3 girls. I pray that God keeps his hedge of protection around them because I know I cannot be around 24/7 throughout their life and even my protection could never be what God can offer. I prayed for a son and Thank you God, I was blessed with a son. A healthy baby boy who is already at the age of 3 is already as much of a gentleman as he is a silly toddler. I love you son. I can remember praying with my wife when she had no clue what direction to go with her hair business. I asked her right then to pray with her an assured her through faithfulness, and work, God would make a way, sure enough, the next day she found a place to begin her journey working for herself as a full-time entrepreneur. Prayer in fatherhood is not just about praying for yourself as a father but also using its power over your family, your wife and children, individually and collectively. Through all this prayer, I believe where the most fall short is the lack of work. The lack of effort and still having to understand our decisions matter. There is no genie, only faith and action. There were times I would pray with no action and have the audacity to ask God why. Those lessons are learned and are still part of life to this day. We must work in tandem with our faith and prayer. Be solid in your decisions and not double-minded. I have been on the ladder and being able to have some self-awareness enables me to recognize when I do operate indecisively. I ought to alert myself and pray for God's forgiveness and guidance. Asking for wisdom to proactively have a better defense for the world's weapons and a spiritual shield for life's transgressions. For me prayer is powerful, prayer is purposeful, prayer is love, and prayer is faithfulness. All of which in some way make up fatherhood.

Dear Lord, as reality reveals to me that no man or family is perfect, I will still praise your name and ask that you guide me as a man, the leader and protector of my family on a righteous path. Please God grant me wisdom and heal my life so that I may provide my family with a good life here on Earth. Amen

ADAPTABILITY & SACRIFICE

ADAPTABILITY – NAVIGATING THE SWIFT CHANGES

"Bae? Bae?" Mom was trying to wake Dad up, the baby was wailing, a newborn beautiful baby girl named Reign.

"Bae!" Mom said with more volume.

"Yea, yea" Dad was a little startled, but he heard the baby crying. "I'm up."

"Can you get the baby, I can't move." Mom tried to get up, but she winced in pain. Dad didn't think much of what she said but immediately got up and went to soothe baby Reign. He knew exactly what was happening. This had happened before, Mom had woken up a few times just last week, unable to fully move. She said that her legs were very heavy and that it hurt to move.

Dad rose slowly, with intention, from the bed trying to shake off the exhaustion of the day before.

"I'm up," he told himself as he yawned. Dad walked over to the crib to soothe Reign.

"Shh, shh, it's ok baby girl," he started to softly sing the melody to the Outstanding by the Gap Band, Reign's favorite song while in the womb. The night was calm, the moon gleaming through the blinds; Lavender filled the air from one of Mom's diffusers, and the baby vibes were just right. Through all this, Dad couldn't help but think about what Mom was going through. It was another night that she woke up with this ailment that neither of them really understood. Each day that Mom awoke with limited mobility, they were forced to adapt and adjust to their day. Dad, while working from home would practice his own form of time management to be productive, at the same time he would increase his workload of housing duties and help Mom a little more with Baby Reign. Mom had just been hired, and her health had suddenly taken a hit, making this transition to new parents one that I guess you could say would make an exceptional story one day. But it was the first-born baby girl that brought a out natural ability to adapt on the fly while still maintaining a positive attitude and optimistic outlook. Still supporting Mom knowing that she was also going through her own mental qualms about her own situation. One that she could not control, a notion that Dad tried to make clear. This adaptation was Dad simply strengthening what was there as a father only this time, in his eyes, his wife's health was so important that it multiplied the magnitude of even the smallest adjustments. From something as simple as feeding the baby to having a meeting hoping and praying that they don't call your name while your beautiful daughter is screaming at the top of her lungs; Dad was more than ready to go full Matrix with anything that life threw at him and his family. He would reach out to his supervisors just to keep a line of communication and because if he ever lost his job due to his duties as an active father in his own situation, at least he knew he would let them know and they just chose not to keep him. Mom needed physical support and emotional support. Providing the physical came easy to Dad. It was the emotional support that required adjusting and again adapting to circumstances out of her and his control. Dad had to learn how to actively listen, tirelessly self-assess his patience, pray, and work unconditionally if he was deeply committed to the love for himself and his family.

Dad changed Reign's diaper all the while still singing and tightly rewrapped her swaddle, she quickly drifted back into sleep. Mom was still in bed, wincing in pain. Trying with all her strength to have some semblance of mobility. It was several months after the birth of the baby, and this was sudden.

"Just relax, lie still, do you need anything?" Dad asked Mom.

"I can't move." Mom tried again to move and became visibly frustrated. Dad, like the times before, felt helpless and was confused, unsure about exactly what was going on or even what Mom meant by not being able to move but as he observed, this time, she literally could not get out of bed. "I hope I'm not having a setback," Dad remembered her saying. A setback Dad learned was what old folks called it when I guess you start to move around too much or do too much after a baby, causing you to get ill.

"Ok, ok, relax I'll call the doctor, or we can go to the emergency room, I'll just contact my job and let them know I can't make it in today." Normally Dad would work from home but tomorrow there was an important meeting where in-person attendance was required. Dad tried to stay calm, even keeled, although he too mentally was having his own setback due to the current state of affairs.

Tears began to swell in Mom's eyes, "It's just too much going on right now," she was trying to hold back the tears as one fell down her cheek. "You are already taking on more and I- I-I'm just tired." Mom had just started a new position, and now she was dealing with this health issue that would certainly keep her out of work and/or she would be in and out while just starting a new job. Dad had made his way back to the bed and held her; He softly kissed her and reassured her of his devotion and faith. They would adapt and evolve. He was not afraid of the challenge. He was committed to his family and his duties as the man of his family.

"Listen, I'm ok, I'm good. This is me. I have no problem combing through the rough with you. I can work from home, you can rest; Reign's ok, we gonna be aight." Dad said.

"Now we gonna take some medicine, let me say a prayer, I'll stay up a little bit longer just in case Reign wakes up." Dad had a little smirk on his face, "But first you gotta get up and do a lil dance." Dad would always try to add some humor in times of adversity and adjustment. Mom knew he could be serious for about 4.5 seconds then it was back to his normal silly self, but she appreciated his efforts. Dad and Mom embraced with a tight hug that lasted for what seemed like forever. Mom laid back down and Dad went back over to the crib just to check on Reign. He felt a sense of calm while looking at his daughter and thought to himself, *now we adapt, we adjust, and we persevere.*

Over time Dad had developed his multi-tasking skills that helped him in adapting to any given situation without any complaints. He was focused on solutions. Over the next couple of months as Mom was recovering from her "setback," all the while starting a new job, Dad was inspired by her resiliency, the feeling was mutual; he discovered he was more than able to take on more to assure everything still ran as smooth as it could just like when Mom was healthy. Dad was discovering that he was adapting to all the changing dynamics surrounding him by being more involved in the care and nurturing of baby Reign, being patient with Mom and her health while supporting the home, keeping a career, and looking to excel. This adaptation would serve him for years to come.

To be adaptable is to be able to adjust to new conditions, being able to be modified for a new use or purpose. I found out very quickly that I would have to adapt at times on the fly. Things could be going very well then flip to a situation I would regard as dreadful.

I remember working from home with my oldest, she was one at the time. While I was in a meeting and she was moving around, she happened to find one of our dog's dried-up turds aaaand ate it. I noticed because after my meeting I went over to give her some attention, "What you over there chewing on?" I picked her up, she had a smile on her face just chewing. "Open," I said, with my eyebrows raised. My daughter enthusiastically opened her mouth. I knew it looked weird; smelled weird, and immediately stuck my finger in her mouth and discovered it was poop. I was scared out of my mind, like aw damn *she's about to get hella sick and it's my fault.* I called my wife, she was calm, but I could tell she was a little worried. So, I rushed to the ER. My wife met me there. I explained to the Dr. what happened, scared out of my mind. I was sure CPS was about to come and investigate. Come to find out, my daughter was fine the whole time. The Dr. had put it plainly. "You're just navigating the ups and downs of being a parent, and you'd be surprised what we see kids get into around here. It was old and no harm." The doctor assured us and even chuckled at how alarmed we were. My daughter was fine, me I was still sweating. But one thing I learned was that as a father there is an immediate instinct to shield your own and you just move into action like autopilot until you feel it's resolved.

Another moment, I am a very playful father then within a blink of an eye I would need to be a protector or comforter. A quick example was at the park one summer during a moment of play and fun, I had to right away, jump into the mind of a protector, comforter, nurturer, and medic. My one-year-old had a febrile seizure on the playground. I had my other 3 kids with me and all I could think about was to stay as calm as possible even though my daughter went limp and was zoned out with a few tremors. I thought I oversaw it well because the kids didn't panic, and I could sense they felt like they could trust me. I called the ambulance and my wife, she left work, met us in the parking lot and we drove to the ER. She was ok, nothing to be readily alarmed about. Just monitor and now we have a better understanding of febrile seizures. It was something my wife had seen in our 5-year-old when she was around 2 also., but that was my first experience and probably the most fearful moment I've had thus far and I can remember adapting on the fly, remaining as calm as possible to not alert my other kids.

Being readily adaptive is something you learn as you experience life. You learn as you get older and wiser; life is always happening. You understand that being able to mold yourself to fit situations as best as you can on the fly is an important skill to have. As a man being adaptable encourages your critical thinking skills and helps you to maneuver through challenges that may arise suddenly in your life with little anxiety and fear. When abrupt changes happen, if you are only responsible for yourself, it is easier to not let it affect you because any decision you make will only affect you. You can decide to act and reshape your thoughts, decisions, or stay the same. As a father, those decisions during sudden changes can affect the family. You must manage with patience and selflessness because a lot of time in fatherhood, adapting leads to sacrifice. For instance, when my wife lost several jobs, this forced me to step up and adapt to a household with one income. This could look like changing budgets, less money for personal pleasure or family pleasures. When my wife was sick, sick to the point where she could barely move, I had to adapt domestically. There was no room for me to expect my wife to manage most of the household duties on her own as she had done in the past. I had to sacrifice some study time or time for my music to take on more but if you are a man operating in true fatherhood you understand how this is important for your family to thrive and to grow. It can also be a shining example for your children to see. Your children are watching your every move. It increases trust between you and your spouse to know that you truly are a team. Being adaptable requires a can-do, will-do attitude instead of a "why do I gotta do" approach.

As a man venturing into fatherhood, I had enough common sense to understand that alterations would have to occur within my life. My lifestyle would need some variation that was conducive to raising a child and being the head of a family. Before I had a family it was wake up, eat, log on to work; at times light me up a jay to get my day started. I was working from home, so I was comfortable, and this made it all too easy to get accustomed to me living a life that was truly just for me; doing what I wanted, when I wanted but still maintaining an employment status, even though growth was stagnant. That is a story for another day. When my lady came into my life nothing really changed all that much, it was just spending that leftover time with another person who I enjoyed sharing space and time with. It came naturally to us. When we found out about our first child things were normal still. But as the pregnancy months passed, I noticed how I was beginning to adapt to the circumstances that unfolded. My purpose was taking shape as the head of the household and father. The man that God intended for me to be. There were moments when I could have something planned, let's say a studio session or even something as simple as "time to myself;" BUT if a situation suddenly happened where I needed to divert my attention elsewhere to be there for my lady and/or child, I would immediately refocus that energy towards them. I know this does not come naturally for others, as for me, my purpose was gradually changing, and I was comfortable with the alterations. For some having to adapt on the fly can be challenging especially if they are still working to figure themselves out and not as foundational sound as they want to be. I can say I was not where I wanted to be financially, spiritually, and mentally but I knew I was in love with this woman and had a vision for our future and wanted a family so when it came to adaptation, I embraced it easier than most. For example, when the mother of your child falls ill to the point where she barely gets out of bed, you take on more responsibilities physically and at the same time increase your emotional support. I struggled with the emotional support, looking back I was not as supportive as I could have been through some tough times, but it wasn't that I didn't want to be, it was more so I am supporting in so many other ways that I felt overwhelmed and pushed to a limit. Being flexible and learning to adapt to change breeds resiliency and as a father and a family man, you must be resilient. As we had more kids, routines had to change but also still maintained those healthy routines which were beneficial when I was just 1 or 2 kids. As we had more children, we had to adapt the routine of bedtime BUT bedtime was still the same, it was important with each child that we steadied the boundary ship when it came to bedtime; it's bedtime and that is mommy and daddy time. You have your own rooms. I believe my kids were able to adapt well because although things were changing, we kept the routine the same. I've learned that kids thrive in routine. When routines must change on the fly, we explain why but once we can get back to that routine we go back. I began to look at adaptation as growth. As things change, I am consistently growing. Mindset and perspective are so important. Rarely ever do I see a moment to be flexible as a negative. I notice the positive reasons for the change and the fortunate outcomes that can arise when unfortunate circumstances present themselves. This adaptation leads me to sacrifice. The next gem that I am still polishing on my fatherhood journey.

CHAPTER

9

SACRIFICE – THE HEART

"Daddy, can we go to Chuck E Cheese, please, please?" Reign had just seen Chuck E Cheese pass by the backseat window. "YES, can we go, can we go!" Marie Lynn shouted.

"Daddy, can we go to Chuck E Cheese?" That was Prince's turn to ask. Dad knew any moment Nicole would be next to ask the same exact question. It never fails, the oldest will ask then in cascade fashion, they all ask the same question. It was a long drive to NaNa house, and he knew there would be even more questions along the way.

"Daddddy, can we go Chuck Cheese?" Sure enough, it was Nicole with the final ask.

"No, nope, nah, and not today," Dad said. "Remember we are having a family Nintendo Night."

"Aww," the kids replied in unison. "But we haven't been in a long time," said Reign.

"Well, we all decided that tonight would be family Nintendo night, so we had to sacrifice another fun adventure, Chuck E Cheese."

"Daddy, what does sacrifice mean?" Marie Lynn asked.

Dad took this as a moment to teach. "Can I tell y'all a story about sacrifice?"

"Yes, yes!"

"Who is Sacrifice?"

"Yes, story, tell us, tell us!"

"I wan' hear sto'y!"

"Ok, so there was once a dad who was a great father and husband. He was an aspiring songwriter/recording artist. He was particularly good at this craft, but Dad was facing a huge challenge of providing for his family while pursuing his dreams. Dad noticed that when he would write outside amongst the stars, he was more inspired."

"What does amongst the stars mean Daddy?" Reign asked.

"It just means he wrote beneath the stars or while the stars were out, or in their presence," Dad replied.

"Oh ok, carry on," said Reign.

Dad chuckled. "Ok so, one restless night, while gazing at the stars, Dad uncovered the magical secret of the stars, they would come alive and share their wisdom with him. They gave him great songs to write, and he felt inspired. Dad became so motivated by the desire to create a better future for his four children, he started to sacrifice his sleep, and personal and family time to meet the divine beings. The stars encouraged him to write amazing songs during these nightly encounters. Dad believed through this demanding work he would create a prosperous life for his family."

"What's pros-prosper-prosperous mean? Marie Lynn struggled to say the word.

"It means wealth, success, financial success," Dad replied.

"Ok, keep going, Daddy."

"Thank you, Marie Lynn. Now as Dad continued to meet late-night with the stars, it was clear that it was taking a toll on his health, and family dynamics. He was struggling to balance his new creativity and his responsibilities as a father and husband. Dad noticed he was exhausted trying to juggle the demands of a day job, a family, a wife, and the desire to give his family the life he dreamed of. He found peace and strength in his music but the strain on his family was forcing him to face the sacrifices he was making. One night as Dad was sitting beneath his starry friends, tired, conflicted, he started to question his decisions. The stars then revealed their heavenly nature, and they told him that they appreciated his selflessness and dedication to being great. In turn they blessed Dad with their special celestial powers, filling him with solace and reassurance. Dad was so pleased that the stars noticed his dedication, he began to take a step back from musical endeavors, understanding the ultimate sacrifice, the importance of spending time with his family and children. His starry friends assured him that his children's future would be wonderful and secure, this allowed Dad to focus more on a healthier balance between pursuing his personal endeavors and being present as a father. Dad began to spend more time with his children, and he shared the songs he wrote with them, encouraging their creativity and teaching them about love and sacrifice. Dad learned that his sacrifice was not in vain, as the blessings he received from the stars ensured a shining future for his family. So, sacrifice is giving up something valued for the sake of something else regarded as more important and worthy. Yall understand now? Kids......."

Dad turned around to see all the kids sleeping.......

All these jewels are very fluid in their makeup. Sacrifice is one we must understand to have successful relationships and a smoother ride on the fatherhood journey. Before my children, one minute you're willing, the next you willing to do whatever it takes to attain, even if your drained, me, myself, and I; but family and fatherhood, if you're a man like I am, it shuts all that shit down. Maybe not initially because pride and ego will fight till, they both win, and one takes over the other. They both can be valuable under certain circumstances, but I've learned that when it comes to fatherhood, pride and ego can drive your decisions. But you notice in either scenario, you ain't winning. For me, my biggest moment of sacrifice was when I decided to stop pursuing my music full-time. If you know me or knew me, you will understand how much time, passion, and devotion I put into my music. I could stay up all night in a studio writing, producing, and recording. I could at the drop of a hat stop anything I was doing and spend hours writing lyrics. There was nothing that could stop me from creating music. Even after 2 kids I was still devoted to pursuing music as a career. Through all the exhaustion that came with being a father of two, pursuing music was still a top priority for me. I believe it was after my baby boy, my third child, that I began to readjust my "why." Our why is the key to why we pursue anything and most of the time, the "why" is driven by personal gain and ego. After my third child was born, I revisited that "why" when it came to a career in music. In the beginning, it was a passion, it was the one thing I did that I could say I did all on my own and was damn good at it. It was the one thing in my life I had total control over, and that the success was tied to how hard I worked and not based on someone giving me a promotion or deciding if the budget was high enough to pay me more. I was driven also by fame and having my name known around the world. When I recorded an album, it was completing a goal but also self-serving. When I readjusted my why, I had to answer the question, how will this help my family short term and long term? I asked the question, how much time would I have available to give to music which required more time than usual and to my family who also were deserving of my undivided time and attention? I had to be real with myself about who I was and how I was built in terms of going all in on my own dreams regardless of anyone else. I came to the realization that I was not willing to give all my time to music even though in the long run it could produce treasures that I could not imagine. But with that pursuit, we all know the chances of that success which I initially yearned for was very slim. I began to think about the practicality of providing for my family short term and long term. I weighed showing my kids that you could chase your wildest dreams no matter what even if that meant Daddy would not be around as much versus going back to school and getting a degree in a high-earning field, which also would allow me to spend more time with my family and be there over the years. I knew initially I would regret or have some resentment towards myself, but I can honestly say I felt none. When I decided to go back to school for Cybersecurity, there was no sense of resentment, there was peace in my decision. A sense of "kingship" knowing that I could sacrifice something I loved so dearly for my family. Even though I sometimes yearn for that studio time and the high that comes from writing your own music and performing, recording, producing; I have not looked back, and I have my BA in Cybersecurity and I am currently in my 2nd year in the field with 2 different roles under my belt. The journey has just begun but I am blessed, and God is clearly showing favor and grace for my sacrifice.

For your children, it would seem easy to sacrifice it all. This is where you start to see the picture a little more clearly. Being a father is like a painting you never finish; because it is forever yours, you are constantly adjusting, editing, and making mistakes. You know you understand that no matter what, by all means necessary I will have a relationship and not a meet and greet with my children.

I remember doing a few things off nothing but impulse. If I wanted something now, I would get it and not think twice about it. Who was it really affecting? Me. Who would suffer the consequences? Me. Until you experience the realization that you are responsible for another human and that humans' decisions throughout life can be traced back to you, it should be a non-factor what you may have to let go to ensure your child has a fighting chance to be the best version of him or herself.

Selflessness was instilled in me from a Christian upbringing. It also felt natural. We as humans can be selfish and non-selfish by nature and I like to think I have done a complete study once all 4 of my kids were present; and I can honestly say when you are young with no life altering responsibilities such as children or a family you can forget what real selflessness feels like. The sacrifice that fatherhood brings includes more than finances. Time is the most asset that we have, and, on this journey, I have learned that my children's only true desire is time with me doing literally anything. It is as simple as rock paper scissors to intense games of Super Mario Brothers; painting outside to having YouTube dance parties. I live for the ice cream trips to Yogurt Land and have four potential Su Chefs that my wife and I can call upon. Sometimes it is a beautiful chaos, a tornado that cleans up after itself, sometimes smiling, sometimes mad; Those moments make the sacrifices worth it. Those moments in time make it more than worth it. If I can sacrifice my time for my children, then I am measuring up as a man. The trick is to still have that hunger for your own ambitions even when your energy may seem low, even when you've spent all you had on the ones you love, you find a way, just a little bit, enough time for yourself; you use whatever time you have left to grow. Sacrifice.

PURPOSE?..MONEY

This is my fatherhood, communication, consistency, discipline, prayer, adaptability, and sacrifice. There is a seventh gem, and it was ironic because 7 is the number of completions. Purpose was that gem. Purpose is essential, with purpose you have direction. Purpose allows for consistent guidance and provides a more stable environment for the entire family. Purpose is the key. Living in your purpose can establish goal setting and your children can see firsthand how their father creates and conquers goals. This teaches children to persevere, and the importance of hard work and dedication. I believed that if my children saw me living in my purpose it would have a positive impact on how they developed in this world. They could see me pursuing my own passions. For example, the first time I played one of my songs for my son, his eyes lit up,

"Daddy that you?" he said.

"Yes, that's me," I replied. After that day, every morning for months before school he would ask to play my songs. When my oldest daughter found out that I was authoring this book, I found her that same night writing a book on her iPad. I told her that if she finished it, I would publish it under our LLC just like Daddy. She has been writing her butt off ever since. Purpose also included resiliency. It is a lot easier to be resilient when you are operating in your purpose or as close to it as possible. When adverse situations arise, you are more likely and willing to bounce back because you have a vision, and you know where you are trying to go. You must want to be resilient; it does not just happen because of the universal ups and downs. Legacy is the residue of purpose. It is the ultimate motivation. It encourages building and supporting traditions and lasting values for generations, ensuring the long-term well-being of your children. It gives you your namesake confidence and pride. To uncover this gem of purpose I had to constantly work on understanding myself, that is the secret to self-liberation, in my opinion, which is purpose.

What could be more fulfilling as a man than truly knowing why you are here on this Earth? What are you doing here? What am I doing here? I've thought about that a lot over all these years of being a father. I can honestly say it feels like I should have been focusing on that earlier in life. Would have a much easier time clearing my head to truly find purpose. When I became a father, I grew to exist in this fortified purpose, being the best father I can be. The best husband I can be. Is that purpose? I am great at it; I also thrive in it but is it my purpose? As a man you often think of your purpose as wealth, power, wealthy family, rich; a common theme, having some type of success that involves money to being the key to freedom. If my purpose is to be the best father and husband that I can be, I'll be at peace and as I get older and wiser I understand what peace truly is. That is part of freedom.

Money. We know the love of it is the root of all evil, but it doesn't mean you don't need it. And I really mean financial literacy. Most of us know how to make some money or create an opportunity to make some but do we really know what to do with it and how to make it work long term; the future in fatherhood may be more important than the past because as you mature as a man you know you can somewhat be prepared for the unpredictable if you have a plan in place for situations as they arise. Money can help control that. You have been pro-active in your fatherhood to always be calm. And to be honest, money helps. Having it, keeping it, creating more opportunities for it, knowing how to grow it. It all matters in fatherhood. I recall Kanye's skits on his college dropout albums about the rich dad and poor dad and the money the rich dad left and the degrees the poor dad left. Of course, it's entertaining but kids cost money, and having it is better than not having it.

After I graduated with my degree in Cybersecurity, I was still at a job that I felt had no growth for me in mind and truly little maneuverability to take my salary where I needed it to go. I had been with a company for about 10 years, and I enjoyed the people, the perks and the working from home. It helped our family dynamics tremendously because daycare is expensive and there is no way we could put all the kids in daycare at the same time. But as the family grew, so did expenses and the need for larger cars, more beds, more clothes, larger clothes, my clothes, wife clothes. We are still working on my clothes and my wife's clothes, but the kids just got new shoes today; we will even that up in a couple of weeks. Anyway, while working at this great company with no growth I had just received my bachelor's degree, so I was applying like crazy to all types of tech jobs. I had no experience in the field whatsoever, but I was so disciplined and consistent with applying; my faith was sky-high and my confidence through the roof. A patience like no other took over and I told myself, *I chose this path, let's go, we rollin until God change out the wheels for wings.* After about 2 weeks of applying through various job boards, I was going through my school emails and saw an email from the career center and their job board. I immediately opened it up and I am quite sure I applied for every job on that job board. Let me tell you that a lot of anxiety went into applying for all these jobs. A couple more weeks had passed, and I had been praying day and night for something to shake because I was just at that point in life where I could feel a shift. I was beginning to feel uncomfortable. For me when I start to feel uncomfortable, usually there is something about to happen in my life, good, bad, or indifferent, but an event may take place that I should prepare for. I should be aware. I was willing to sacrifice that time I get working from home with my kids to go into an office full time if that meant I made the money that I needed to provide the life I wanted for my family. But I had to be careful about saying what "I wanted." I need to pray be patient and listen to what God wants. I had to put my faith into action and not just talk about it. Live it and operate in faith and work. About 28 days had passed since I graduated, and I landed my first interview as a Security Analyst. I was back in study mode. The discipline I had learned over the years as a father brought me to this point where I would always be initiative-taking and prepare for any type of interview, whether I have experience or not. I would research the description and find keywords. I would write down notes on legal pads and sticky notes. I would memorize key points of the job descriptions and posts. I made sure to know a couple of key facts about the company. What's funny about all this is that half of the material that I studied didn't even come up in the interview. But I don't care, I just like to be disciplined and prepared. And that preparedness paid off because I aced the first interview and in the 2nd interview, 75% of what I studied they asked about. That discipline and preparation had paid off. If you haven't heard it, I'll say it, *Proper Preparation Prevents Poor Performance.* Just 24 hours after that 2nd interview I received a call that said I had been offered the position. I was so excited and thankful to God for this opportunity. I was blessed to have this job in my field fresh out of school. After I received the offer letter, I noticed a small sacrifice that I would have to make. The salary that I was looking for was not there, in fact, it was only a few thousand a year higher in salary, nowhere near what I had envisioned. What is interesting is that I had another job that was offering more money but not in the tech industry at all. I went back and forth between the two companies. I even tried to negotiate. Neither would budge and I understood. After much consideration, prayer, and communication with my wife I decided to go with the job in my career field. I was anxious because this was the beginning of that day when I decided to change my life trajectory and go back to school. I was excited because I felt at peace with my decision, and it felt like I was heading in the right direction.

After working as a security analyst for about a year, I was moved into a different department with vulnerability management. I had asked for a transfer to a new team because my analyst position required more on-call, 24/7 availability.

Add the family aspect and the pay, I had to take a personal stand and ask for them to meet me halfway. My supervisor was understanding and eventually found a spot for me on another team. I must pause right here and say God has really blessed me to have superiors who have always wanted to see me grow and respected me as a man and employee. When I accepted the new role, I thought it would come with some type of raise. I was dead wrong. Even though it was a more challenging role with a greater customer focus and reporting sensitive data with round-the-clock meetings. It gave me more time and ability to hone my leadership skills and speak directly to executives and stakeholders. I loved the job, the team, and the tools I used. I knew that it would be of some use even if there was no pay increase, BUT I was going to find me another job, so for about a whole year, I was applying for jobs; I was taking training, I revamped my resume about 4, 5, 6, 789 times. I was starting to get that feeling of discomfort. Life was changing again, my kids were getting older, bills were getting higher, and my salary was not keeping up with the times. I must have gone on at least 5 in-person interviews about 2 to the final round, ending in nos. Hundreds of phone interviews, all no. I was praying, sacrificing time, practicing discipline, trying to stay patient and wait on my time while adapting to life itself; my wife had to shut down her salon suite, bills were higher, kids needed clothes again and just life in general was forcing me as a father to adjust and adapt constantly. I was consistent as ever in doing a certain number of applications a day. I did my best to communicate with my wife and kids when Daddy needed to study and communicate with my job about childcare and working from home. I remember feeling like *Man I am extremely uncomfortable right now, God you must be doing something or it's some REAL DEAL bad shit about to happen.* I was having chest pains at some points during this hunt for a better opportunity. I knew I had earned it, I deserved it. My momma has said time and time again, *you are in favor.* After thousands of applications, hundreds of hours of self-training, plenty of no's, delinquent payments, near disconnection notices. I received a call about a job offer from a smaller company for an in-person interview. It was not in my field of cyber security, but it was in IT. I didn't know what to think or really what it meant but like I always do. I went in with full optimism and faith. I went ahead and asked them what are some things that I might need to know in advance. I went and did my research and focused on the key concepts in the job description. My first interview was a success. I could feel it as soon as I walked in. The confidence and preparation that I had felt like it was years in the making. The next day I was at once called for a 2nd interview. The 2nd interview was a little more challenging but again I walked away feeling better than I have ever felt. All the things that I had learned subconsciously while working at jobs where I was burnt out or not valued, like being a leader, collaborating, and processes rolled off my tongue during questioning in the 2nd interview. If you pay attention, lose some pride, and humble yourself, you can always find a flower around a bunch of shit. I was so anxious over the next several days because I had not heard from them. I was beginning to doubt communication, consistency, discipline and patience, adaptability, and sacrifice. I was beginning to doubt my faith. I had to pray and ask God to keep restoring my faith and forgive my fear and my doubt. About 4 days after the 2nd interview, I received a call that said I had been offered the position with a 40% increase in salary with the possibility of a raise after 6 months. It was in the office, but it was about 20 minutes closer than the primary office of the current company. I had made another sacrifice but for everything great, something good must be lost. As soon as I got off the phone, without delay, I started praising God. I know I looked like Will Smith in Pursuit of Happyness. It felt like a relief, like I had finally stepped into another chapter of Fatherhood. I could provide and strive instead of provide and survive. I could start to build that foundation that had cracked so many times, sometimes from my own doing. All these gems that I had discovered over the years had brought me here to this moment. This moment I share with you.

In the end all these 7 gems all contribute to my growth as a father and all of them if you read between the lines intertwine with one another. To be able to adapt you must sometimes sacrifice. When you sacrifice you must be patient to see the fruit that was born. When you sacrifice you practice discipline to support that sacrifice and you discipline out of love, but you must be consistent in your discipline with yourself and your children who need different forms of communication that also must be loving and patient. Communication through prayer is crucial because not only can you ask God to help you work on each of these 7 gems, but you can also teach your kids the importance of communication through prayer. This comprehensive approach has helped alleviate any extra headaches, anxiousness, doubt, and fear on my fatherhood journey. If I stop and assess fatherhood, I can find one of these 7 gems in any situation and act accordingly to practice them correctly.

Fatherhood is really the best hood and I thank my mother for even mentioning that I should draft a book about my journey as a father back in her kitchen 4 years ago. I want to thank my wife for pushing me to finish and even get started and believing in a vision. I want to thank my kids for being more than inspiration and motivation, more than my why, but the engine under the hood of being a father. My babies mean more than the world to me, and this book is dedicated to them. I want to thank my dad for always keeping it one hundred when it came to our convos about being a man and father. I gotta thank God for blessing me with the gift and passion for writing. It's not rhymes but this takes me back to when I was a kid writing stories and poems. Thank you, God, for still guiding me on this fatherhood journey and being with me every step of the way. Fatherhood is not for the weak and it's more than money. Fatherhood is the best hood and I want to give all my brothas in this hood a special shout-out, take care of our ladies, and take care of your babies, God Bless.

End

THANK YOU, RODGERS FAMILY

FATHERHOOD